USING A SMARTPHONE - A GUIDE FOR SENIOR CITIZENS.

In simple steps you will learn about the functions and applications on your Android smartphone.

By

James Sparkling

CONTENTS

1. INTRODUCTION.

Dear Reader!

This guide has been written for seniors who have problems with using their android smartphone. If you don't feel up to it and you don't use the full functionality of your smartphone because no one has explained to you, dear reader, the possibility that lies in a small but very useful and clever device - THIS GUIDELINE IS FOR YOU - I present in it a simple way how to use your smartphone. A few easy and pleasant steps will explain - what and how. This is the perfect time for you to take your smartphone in your hand and here we go! You will have an interesting journey through discovering the functions hidden in your device.

I. INTRODUCTION TO THE SMARTPHONE'S EXTERNAL CONTROL.

1. THE BUTTONS ON YOUR SMARTPHONE.

In the newest smartphones there are usually two buttons usually on the right side there is a POWER button which means switching on or waking up the device. The button to turn on or wake up the device can be located on the right or left side of the device. When you press the upper part of the button, the sound will be heard and when you press the lower part of the button, you will turn the device off. Depending on the model and manufacturer of the device there are only these two keys, there may be, for example, another button to mute or turn on the sound in the device - it is usually on the left side, but in some phones it may be so called Bixby, its operation can be changed - at your discretion it may be a voice assistant or you can assign the application. In the newest smartphones it usually does not exist, but in older models there is a button under the screen in the middle which is used to wake up the smartphone/reverse to the main desktop/unblock the smartphone with a fingerprint. This of course depends on the smartphone model.

I. INTRODUCTION TO THE EXTERNAL OPERATION OF THE SMARTPHONE.

2. SLOTS IN THE SMARTPHONE.

The most important input in your smartphone is the cable entry from the charger. Depending on the model of the phone and the appropriate charger - we distinguish USB type C, i.e. the plug can be connected with any side, USB type micro, the plug can be connected with only one, matching side. These two chargers and sockets are most popular, although they are different. The next input, which is not always the case, is the so-called 3.5 mm Mini Jack. It is used to connect headphones.

I. INTRODUCTION TO THE EXTERNAL OPERATION OF THE SMARTPHONE.

3.GENERAL CONSTRUCTION OF MODERN TOUCH PHONES.

In the front there is of course a screen, I recommend to buy a protective glass on it to protect the screen from being smashed. Another thing is the front camera for taking pictures of the so called "selfie", next to it there is also a loudspeaker for conversations and an invisible light sensor. There may be a house button on the lower one but it does not have to be. At the back of the device there is a camera, sometimes there is also a fingerprint reader in the middle. On the sides of the device, there are in various layouts:

- power button,

- buttons for subduing / muting the device,

- Some have a Bixby button,

- Not always, but you may find the button responsible for mute your smartphone,

- tray with sim / memory card,

- speaker (usually at the bottom),

- microphone - at the bottom of the device,

- charging connector,,

- headphone cable entry.

Possible but not necessary, but certainly a similar layout of buttons and sockets on the smartphone.

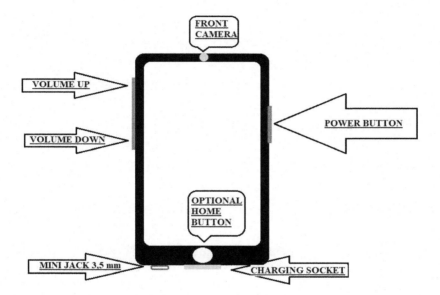

II. INTRODUCTION TO THE INTERNAL SERVICE.

1. UNLOCKING THE SMARTPHONE.

To unlock the smartphone we press the power button, usually it is on the right side. It is possible to unlock through the fingerprint reader. When the screen turns on, depending on the lock - simply move the padlock, enter the PIN and confirm or draw the previously set shape. Generalizing to enter or change the type of the screen lock - enter the settings, then choose the lock screen (usually this is how it is called), there you can change the lock to PIN, shape, password, fingerprint or even face detection.

II. INTRODUCTION TO THE INTERNAL OPERATION.

2.MOVING AROUND THE INTERFACE.

After unlocking the smartphone by moving sideways, you have access to desktops where you can place applications and widgets to run them quickly. On the bottom bar of the screen we have buttons such as home (usually in the middle), undo (i.e. the left arrow), and a list of recently opened applications (usually three vertical dashes). By moving up at the bottom of the screen, or by clicking the icon at the bottom, you have access to all installed applications. When you press an application, it turns on. On the main desktop - when you move the top of the screen towards the bottom you have access to the place where there are notifications and access to quick start of device functions. These include Wi-Fi, Bluetooth, Mobile Data, Flashlight, Airplane Mode, Screen Rotation Lock. After moving down again there are more functions, we move between them by moving right or left. To add an application to the start screen you have to hold down an application in the list of applications and either a balloon with options will be displayed, or if you hold down an application for a longer time, it will move to the main screen.

III.SUPPORT BASIC APPLICATIONS OF EACH SMARTPHONE.

1.CONTACTS.

To enter the contacts, click the icon, and you have access to the contact list. In the latest smartphones just move to the right to make a call. In older models, you need to enter the contact and click on the phone stamp.

To add a contact you have to press the plus, which is displayed on the right, it is sometimes on the top and sometimes on the bottom, depending on the device.

Touching at the bottom or top you have access to the last calls and to the phone/keyboard. In the last calls we have a list of people we have called chronologically, with the time and date given. Going to the phone/keyboard we can dial the number to which we want to call and approve it through the green phone handset. The phone can also be used to recharge the phone if we have a card agreement.

III.SUPPORT BASIC APPLICATIONS OF EACH SMARTPHONE.

2.MESSAGES.

By touching the icon of the message you have access to the possibility to write a message through the icon or plus. We also have a list of people with whom we have exchanged SMS messages. After clicking on a given conversation, you can read or write a message by clicking on the bar at the bottom, the keyboard appears.

III.SUPPORT BASIC APPLICATIONS OF EACH SMARTPHONE.

3.CAMERA.

After touching the camera icon, the camera image is displayed. The circle at the bottom takes a picture. The arrows next to it change the camera to the one in front of the device, on the other side from the photo trigger wheel there is an icon, when you click it, it takes you to the last photo in the Gallery. Additionally, in the upper part there are different functions from flash settings (lightning) - on, off, automatic. There is a self-timer setting, proportions, filters and settings that can be changed with the sprocket in the upper left corner (each setting is described there in detail and depends on the model).

There is also a recording function, i.e. video, and you can still turn on the pro camera version, take panoramic pictures, take pictures at night in low light, record a movie in slow or very slow motion or, for example, take food pictures. There is also an option to take pictures in wide-angle and normal mode, you can find an option to run a scenery optimizer. Of course, these functions and many others occur depending on the smartphone model.

III. SUPPORT FOR BASIC APPLICATIONS OF EACH SMARTPHONE.

4.CLOCK AND ALARM CLOCK.

In the Clock application you can immediately open the list of alarm clocks that you have previously set. To add an alarm clock, press on the plus sign, which is usually in the upper right corner. Next to the plus sign we have three dots, after clicking on them we can remove the alarm clocks from the list, change the settings or use the help. When you click on the plus sign, the interface opens where you have: time for which you want to set the alarm; days of the week; name of the alarm; sound of the alarm; vibration; snooze. When you click on the alarm sound, vibration, snooze, you can change these parameters and to turn them off/on, click the slider on the right of each setting. At the bottom we have two options - cancel and save, so of course to set the alarm click save. When you go to the alarm main page, where the list of alarms is, you have at the bottom or at the top functions such as: time in the world, where you can see what time is currently in some place in the world, and to add a new city, click the plus; then there is the stopwatch; the last function is the timer.

III.SUPPORT BASIC APPLICATIONS OF EACH SMARTPHONE.

5.GALLERY.

In the gallery of our device you will find photos, videos, pictures or videos downloaded from the Internet and screenshots. You probably know most of the listed possibilities of the gallery content, but you don't know what a screenshot is, it is taken at practically any time of everything that is on the screen - for example: something we have been looking for on the Internet and want to save it in the gallery. The screenshot is taken by, depending on the model, if there is a physical key underneath the screen, you have to press it together with the power key, otherwise you have to press the silence button and the power key. After entering the Device Gallery we have a list of the above mentioned images. In the lower or upper bar we have the Images - that is, the list of images chronologically, followed by Albums - sorted images located in the smartphone - albums can be camera photos, screenshots, downloaded files and others. You can create an Album with three dots in the upper right corner, after clicking on it there is a list where you can create a new album. Next in the bar is history and sharing, where we can create a shared album for example for our family.

III.SUPPORT BASIC APPLICATIONS OF EACH SMARTPHONE.

6.CALENDAR.

In the calendar app we have access to the calendar presented in a chosen way year, month, week. On particular days we can set events by double-clicking or once by clicking on the date and on the plus displayed in the bottom right corner of the device. Then you will see a desktop with the title of the event, the time of beginning and end of the event, the place, notes, and invitees. After moving to the right, the next month appears in the monthly calendar view, and to see the previous month you have to move to the left. By clicking on the name of the month you can check the selected month of the selected year. It is intuitive simply by using the arrows to move the year, and from the list of months we select and click on the month of interest. Clicking the date icon in the upper left corner of the screen marks the current day. After clicking the three lines in the upper right corner of the screen, the list is displayed where you can set the calendar view for the year/month or synchronize the calendar with your other calendars, for example, with e-mail.

III.SUPPORT BASIC APPLICATIONS OF EACH SMARTPHONE.

7. WEB BROWSER.

After starting the web browser, a window appears in which we can search for something by clicking on the bar with the following text: search or enter the address and enter the desired password. After clicking on the right and left arrows on the bar, we move the viewed pages forward and backward (these are 1st and 2nd in the barshot below). The House button is used to undo the browsing to the beginning (this is 3rd on the bar), the star button is used to create and synchronize bookmarks in different browsers (this is 4th on the bar). If you have already searched for something and want to have it opened quickly the next time you click the tab icon (square-shaped) in the bottom or top bar (this is 5th on the bar). The icon of the three horizontal bars calls up a list of other functions such as: downloaded files; browsing history; saved pages; share; dark mode; ad blocking; computer version; text size; add-ons; print; settings (this is 6 on the bar).

IV. SEARCHING AND INSTALLING APPLICATIONS.

With the google play application we download the necessary applications. From this store we download practically all possible applications and games. These are among others: Facebook, Twitter, YouTube, Instagram, Messenger and other useful applications, there are also games there. In order to download an app, you enter the google play store and search for the app using the search bar, which is always at the top of the screen and says: search for apps and games. Then, after clicking on this text, the keyboard is shown and you type the name of the application and click on the magnifying glass or search, then the list of applications is shown, click on the icon of the application you are looking for and the text is installed on a green background. After downloading and installing, the application is in the list of applications previously discussed, but I will repeat it for your convenience. After leaving the startup screen, move your finger from the bottom of the screen to the top, or if it is an older model, click the button at the bottom of the bar. If there is no downloaded application, move your finger to the right of the screen and finally find it. On the page of a given app in the google store we have screenshots of it; description of the app; ratings and opinions of this app; comments; similar apps and other related apps. All the above mentioned content is in order from top to bottom. In the google play store itself, there are tabs under the search bar, such as: for you, top lists, paid, categories, family, our choice. I think you don't need any more comment, all these bookmarks according to the description, when you click on a given suggest an application that we can download and install on our smartphone. At the top search bar there is also a microphone icon on the right, after clicking on it we can say what we want to search instead of writing. To the left of the search bar there are three horizontal bars that expand the list of functions: my games and applications, notifications, wish list, account, etc

Printed in Great Britain
by Amazon

27742678R00020